Darling, Dad-Poems after you.

Nazia Koser

India | USA | UK

Darling, Dad-Poems after you. © 2024
Nazia Koser

All rights reserved.

No part of this publication may be reproduced, stored in a retrieval system, or transmitted, in any form or by any means, electronic, mechanical, photocopying, recording or otherwise, without the prior written permission of the presenters.

Nazia Koser asserts the moral right to be identified as author of this work.

Presentation by *BookLeaf Publishing*

Web: www.bookleafpub.com

E-mail: info@bookleafpub.com

ISBN: 9789360941871

First edition 2024

Mohammed Aslam Mir and Jamila Begum, my world, my rock and my all.

ACKNOWLEDGEMENT

A many thanks to my husband for your patience and support. Massively in awe of my amazing children, thank you for all your love, care and unwavering belief that I can do anything I want to. I believe that for you too.

PREFACE

21 poems by Nazia Koser,
A daughter, sister, wife, mummy, teacher and friend.
A poem for when I miss you, think of you, celebrate and grieve; my darling daddy. My Abbhaji.

A leaf falling.

Sway, swish, and swing.
It falls on the ground with a hush,
Leaving a sweet sound, a ring.
The leaf lay sprawled in the magnificent mush.

Come call me oh sweet leaf
I will attend your every need,
As it is time to show and shine your belief.
Gently I will care and caress your every silent need.

Alas, I hear no sound, no magic, no laughing, no wish
Where is your might, your light and spark,
I look up, I see you sturdy and strong yet almost finished
Come back I plead; one more trip to the park.

Oh leaf, leaf so beautiful, so kind and caring,
Your life so green and daring.
How you lay so peaceful and fulfilled,
I am done you say. I am thrilled.

Going up a mountain.

Step by step I heave, I heave, I grasp I grab.
This trek will kill me, I say. Do I stop though?
Why is this so tough, so gruelling, so hard.

I muster my courage-be brave they say.
These breaths are too weary, I say, Do I sit though?
Why is this so tough, so gruelling, so hard.

Grab on, hold tight, I slip a little- I relapse.
Is the air changing, a chill I say, Do I go slower though?
Why is this so tough, so gruelling, so hard.

A blur is all I can see as I look back. It's all a blur.
Keep going, time is the key, they say. Do I go run though?
Why is this so tough, so gruelling, so hard.

Move on, speed up, don't slow down. I hear the words.
The weight on my back is getting heavier, I say.

Drop the bags and keep going, they say. Do I leave it all behind though? Why is this so tough, so hard.

The air is lighter, hours have passed. What a scene!
The peak is near, the end is nearer. Am I really there, I say? I see the layers of stone, the smooth, the rough and the sharp cracks. My eyes close, I sigh and breath in.
This is the ease, the peace, after the hard as they said.

Folding clothes.

Shirts, trousers, skirts, dresses and socks
What am I missing? Underwear and the frocks?
Or the jumpers and cardigans, maybe the tops?
Towels and dishcloths thrown in I see
Washing clothes is a calming thing, gathering
the loads and piling them separately according to
the person, then I call and they collect, I start
over the very next day
This is smooth and edgy though, the velvety feel
crushed from years of wear. So pretty and dense
and precious
Oud oozes still on the long shirt, a Friday
favourite I know
Why this one though? Palish grey and subtly
blue the cotton creases as I pressed down and
fold. My shaky caress engraves the creases as
my fingers run rapidly over the long shirt, this
sweet-smelling shirt. Daddy was this yours?
He wore it that day, the day was a Friday, they
day he last went out to the mosque. I folded that
shirt today, for the last time, during the day, the
last time today as I washed and folded the
clothes today

Choosing a coat.

Today is the day I buy a new coat, is this true mummy?
Can it be the day, I waited so long for a day like today.

It has to be perfect, mummy, just perfect can it be?
Long, I think, maybe blue, dark or even black, perhaps grey?

Eight buttons, maybe more, sixteen even, can I have more?
Smooth and sturdy, what does that even mean mummy?

My new coat is waiting for me, lets go mummy, why wait?
With pockets all over I need an inner one too, secretly.

Perhaps a hood, definitely fur around the neck.
Warm and toasty: Cozy and homely, is that a thing?

My new coat mummy will be just for me, just for me?
Wrap it around me to see if the coat wants me mummy?

I chose my new coat today; it chose me too.
I wore it today to the charity shop.
My new coat and me, are happy, thanks mummy.

Mind. Memory. Tears.

Tiny, miniscule variants of thought push and persuade
in a frenzy to get seen to get past all the haze.

Exposing, uncovering, displaying the specks ready to ignite
the towering, cowering, spewing wave of wet to be set free.

Mind and memory magical and mighty holding tight with
might and so majestic in its grandeur, so heavenly light.

Trembling and shivering and quivering they tumble
accidently spoiling and uncoiling the path the way.

Teary tears are so gentle and unblemished sneakily private
forcefully yet true and brutally soothing and calmly blessed.

Repeatedly then the mind whispers to the
memory a spark a
truth alerting the tears to come and rescue me
from you.

Reading a newspaper.

Read he said.
Read every word, he said.
So I read and he told.
The man is a liar, he shouted out.
He painted the town in red with his words.
Read on.
The money is coming, for the poor and children.
What a croc! They said that before, he screamed.
Read more. The pot needs to grow, so we can build.
The pot needs more so we can sustain.
They fumble with the pot, where is it today.
What a bunch of liars he said, oh the spew!
Read more and more. Is that not enough, I say.
No, there's more as always there's more.
Three more stores will close, more jobs are gone.
No more milk driven to the door or eggs.
Was to come, he said, this time, was to come.
Prices rise again dad. I know, they do and not the packet though never the packet only the bank.
Oh dad let's forget this and tell me about abroad.
No more said dad, about here or abroad. Be honest all is all.

The party.

The light is lightning.
It flashes and blinds them all.
The music sirens the warning unheard and missed.
Life is a party.

If that was the truth, then how come I dance not.
If that was the truth, then how come she screams in pain.
If that is true, then why is it dark so early every day?
Life is a party.

Boom, boom, boom again. Swell so the walls in pain.
Slowly trickle down the tears on the face.
Sincerely it sounds like just some beat old yet it toils the time I was blue. Not again nothing new.
Life is a party, I hear.

Talk is crammed in time to the beats of the drum.
Scurrying words trying to get in edge ways.
Meanwhile, I

Hear the screech and the thump. The siren and the clench.
Dirty and red was the note they said. All is quiet, now.
Really, life is a party, that said, so it is thin thread bare.

Homeland-foreign.

Running like a rat unwanted and done.
Skipping like a cat kindred and true.
Bouncing like a ball from here to there.
Jumping like a kanga with minutes to spare.
Crouching like a cricket on a branch bare.
Balancing like a breeze in mid-air.
Creasing like a lizard sun burnt and austere.
Screaming like a swimming bear with a sore head.
Climbing out like a prince with slicked back hair.
Gushing like a river with dare.
Standing tall like a man with valour and flare.
Juggling like a circus freak ignoring the threats and treats.
Hiking like a true entrepreneur all the will and ware.
Strolling like a picturesque hare unaware.
Plunged like a thumping ache as you lay awake.
Clutching like a lost bird to its lair and young.
Grasping like fish out in the ocean for air.
Strutting like a soldier its silverware. Finally
Smiling like a foreign spare now home, happy and a prayer.

Seeds and growing.

Tiny seeds
In the soil
The hole is
Dug watered
And rugged
There you lay
Oh mighty seed
Grow and thrive
Big and might
Not slight
But strong and
Tight the branches be
When the wind blows
Stand thee the
Push and shove
Grow tiny, tiny seeds
Soak in the sun
Brush past the pest
Quiver and quake
When the rain
Pounds down
And angers your ground.
Seed so blessed
Let out
Your spirit so true

Of how to ignore
The shaky shouts
Screaming shouts
Wailing in
The wind swaying
Gently nudging
You to die.
Seed ignore it
Grow just grow
I urge you to
Mature smooth
Lightly stand
On the dirt
It blew
Just for you
The dust calls
Seed for you
To grow and glow true.

Relatives.

Strangers alert ha!
Chit and chat-here and there. Where?
Gone. Not to be seen.

Forewarned beware
The bite is not bare just sly
Marked forever then.

Wounds are dusted then
Wrapped in forbidden dirt
Then ripped from me.

I bear clear now, stop.
Hurt no-one no more forever
Tides can break too.

Dream untimely and dare
Be different just don't care. Yeah!
Now it ends the rancour.

Heritage.

There it stands, tall and elegant the beautiful unique picture of us all.
The slithery lines of water colour smudged so finely all fades under the crease.
Mine is stark-the vision-I see he, she, they and them shoulder to shoulder so strong.
The slight lean and slight look at those sat down so graciously and anxious on the floor.
Children so beautifully combed and clothed how grand you look. The pride. The honour. The heritage.
Brown and dark brown and brown again. So deeply distraught as how we became blue.
Who is the blue-eyed babe? Untrue are the tales of uncertainty-questions must rise, he says.
Oh painting, grand painting speak tell me your tale. Where were you written, then hidden, then escaped.

Eating an ice-cream.

Cold and clear-ice-creams are great, to eat in the cold.
Your first is the best and then even better again.
Chilly candy or chocolate chip-enjoy the treat.

Mountains of millions on top.
So colourful and true.
Mine is mint.

Dripping down the side the sweet stickiness escapes.
Pay the man, dad, he calls quick.
A cone and tub a lollipop too.

Ice-creams are a treat in the cold.
Everyone watches the silly us.
Do we care? We lick and lick and lick.

Dad the ice-creams you bought were the best.
They were fun, fresh and fair.
Ice-creams are best in the warm too.

The funfair.

I do like to go to the funfair, I do.
The noise the smell the swears.
Bright and beautiful-so new.

I do like to go to the funfair, I do.
The coins justle in pockets and add up.
Bright and beautiful-so new.

I do like to go to the funfair, I do.
Swinging round and round, feeling dizzy to the ground.
Bright and beautiful-so new.

I do like to go to the funfair, I do.
Higher and higher the carriage carries me across.
Bright and beautiful-so new.

I do like to go to the funfair, I do.
Swishing and swaying my bones this way and that.
Feeling bruised and blue-not so new.

Fish and chips.

I just love fish and chips, don't you?

Crispy and crunchy the fish is oily.

I just love fish and chips, don't you?

It pours the rain so fast and furious.

I just love fish and chips though, don't you?

Daddy stops at the corner place, three bags please.

I just love fish and chips today, don't you?

Vinegary, saltish and mushed: chips are the best.

I just love fish and chips every day, don't you?

Newspaper wrapped and squashed together, just us.

I just love fish and chips always, don't you?

Shopping.

Cards ready. Cash in purse. Off we go. Shops galore.
Shoes and bags and clothes. That's the list. Get the gist?

First shop. Dresses and more. Blue please, that is a tease.
Then to stop at a paper shop. Bags and glue for my old shoe.

Shopping malls so big and daring. I feel lost needing toast.
Pushing past the crowds. The skirt is new. I want it too.

I pay and carry; oh the bags are mighty. Ready and steady.
Still not enough money spent. Need more. Do I? Sure.

Ravishing red top calls out for me to stop. I obey, just pay.
Shoes, shoes I hear you begging. I am on my way, wait, pray.

Too tired and tipsy. I stop for a break. The bank is broke.
So to home I go and wear and stare in the mirror I spoke.

Shopping done; money gone. Maybe this can find someone.
These old shoes and clothes need to be gone.

The sunshine.

Stunningly ecstatic it towered above all.
Spreading its valour, velvet feely fingers across
the lawns. The tired tips on the teary bushes
stand upright as the sunshine makes its call.
Wake up, wake up, it is the time, time to pray.

Majestically savouring all particles available, its
dust is urging more. Shining protrude distance
yet closing the unearthly linger as exposed. The
sunshine squeals in delight so prim and precise.
Wake up, wake up, it is the time, time to pray.

Hide, quick take shade, hear it comes, the
monster is back.
She shouts, he shouts, they all run about. It came
mamma it came so bright. So bright, brutal and
betrayed. The sunshine kills and covets all it
sees. We hide and it hales.
Run, run, run away as it comes again to destroy.
Please pray.

Every tip, every taunt, every unbelievably dried
thorn squeal and squirm as the sunshine enthrals.
'We see you; we feel you; we know you' say the
small, we cry, we scream, we fear.

Run, run, run away as it comes again to destroy.
Please pray

Spring onions.

Jiggle and jump.   The spring onions are done.
          Long greenish stems ready to be snipped.
Flavouring the dish is best when garnish sings.
          Sings does the song the new bird whistle.
Wiggle and waggle.   Ready to uproot and wash.
          Slightly silly are the stems in the sun.
Constantly acidic, politely prose.   The springs are the one.
   And misty it appears the sky agrees the tone a bit bleak.
          Sparkling daringly white invite the sturdy ends.
The spring onions ready to be friends.
          Caressed and now ripe they call for a flight.
Get us out they shout.   Have us today, snip, snip away.
          The spring onions are done.
Up arose the sun, debating whether to stare.
     Ignoring all the signs its spring, I swear.

Calling all knights, come out, come out. It is time to fight.

As the time has passed and the spring onions are done.

Graveyards.

Colour intrigues me. What colour is me?
I like the graveyard. It calls me tonight.
Dull, dreary and dark. Yet it is me.
I love the graveyard. It bellows my name.
Brown, black and grey. Yet it is me.
I adore the graveyard. It shouts out my name.
Yellowy, pale and cream. Yet it is me.
I admire the graveyard. It hollers at me.
Pinkish, rosy and plush. Yet it is me.
I appreciate the graveyard. It shrieks at me.
Reddish, magenta and rouge. Yet it is me.
I value the graveyard. It roars at me.
Blue, turquoise and navy. Yet it is me.
I respect the graveyard. It almost growls at me.
Grassy, muddy and green. Yet it is me.
I implore the graveyard. It sometimes snarls at me.
Naked, nude and true. Yet it is me.
I am with the graveyard. It called and became me.
I liked the graveyard. It coloured me.

Terminally.

So tired I am of losing you, again I say goodbye, daddy.
They tell me you are ill, terminally.

My eyes are wet, slimy and sore, I cry a river, I cry the storm. I know you are ill, just terminally, am I sure?.

So hard it is, daddy to conceive this all. They said that's it. You have no more time. Why is it so, why terminally, is all.

I gather my breath; I gather my gall. I want to spew I want to scream for sure. A few hours they said though that's all we knew. How can you be terminally ill, Abbhaji?.

It hurts, it scorches, the deep plunge has all control. I am alone, I see all alone. How can you be so ill, so done, only terminally or?

I prepared. I did. I held on again to it all. I swore, I loved you with my all. Don't leave us daddy, we begged. We knew though, we just knew. Daddy would be no more, for he would leave us, terminally, just terminally that's all. See you soon, see you again. Never terminal never all.

Rose-coloured.

I wear glasses. I wear rose-coloured glasses.
They shimmer and shine, and mine they are all mine.
I see everything I am meant to see then I switch to the mysterious lens I have stored within me.
I wear them on the brim of my nose, if you look closer, they yell they call. Come join me, and be in my rose-coloured world.
The sun shines, not bright but beyond kindly. The rain descends not bogged but divine. The snow falters not deep but scrumptious. Come join me, I dare you, to be in my rose-coloured world.
I wear them hidden on the tip of my nose; can you imagine? The drama and dread when called to defend. The fire spreads not dangerously but dreamily. The winds waves not howls as it may all end. It is serene here where I am, come on be with me in my rose-coloured world.
They giggle and gurgle not silent and dead. The babes glisten ethereally not neglected and denied. I am aware, I saw. I will again call you all again. Stop and secure.

Be amicable and share this rose-coloured world with me, in my glasses I see, the place I plead the world to be.

I hear-hope.

I hear and hope you will love me, as I love thee.
My hugs I line with lining so deep in luxury.

Any moment now the rise will come, so peaceful.
Elegantly skim across the sandy place, graceful.

Calmly and quaint as the wave catches its glee.
I squirm with warmth in that moment for you to see.

Chirping silently the dove cooed a different melody.
I am aware as my heart skipped and danced cleverly.

That it is not the song or sea which delves so deep
I beat and vibrate with love and I could over heap.

The cage against it all seems so weak and failing
Am I stop feeling, smiling, gleaming and craving?

It is you, who is hope. I hold so dear to me
I hear and hope you will love me, as I love thee.
My hugs I line with lining so deep in luxury.

Milton Keynes UK
Ingram Content Group UK Ltd.
UKHW012311160324
439511UK00013B/358